The life cycle of a
Salmon

Ruth Thomson

WAYLAND

First published in 2006 by Wayland
an imprint of Hachette Children's Books

British Library Cataloguing in Publication Data
Thomson, Ruth
    The life cycle of a salmon. - (Learning about life cycles)
    I. Salmon - Life cycles - Juvenile literature
    I Title
    571.8'1756

Editor: Victoria Brooker
Designer: Simon Morse
Senior Design Manager: Rosamund Saunders

Printed and bound in China

Hachette Children's Books
A division of Hodder Headline Limited
338 Euston Road, London NW1 3BH

Photographs: Page 1 and 20 © 2006/Grant
Klotz/AlaskaStock.com; 2 and 6 Don Mason
/CORBIS; 4-5, 7, 10 and cover (top); 11 Jeff
Foote/naturepl.com; 8 Michael Quinton/Minden
Pictures/FLPA; 9 Brandon D. Cole/CORBIS; 12 and
cover (centre right), 16, 17 and 23 © 2006/Mark Emery/
AlaskaStock.com; 13 and cover (bottom) Michael Sewell/
Still Pictures; 14 Gunter Marx Photography/CORBIS; 15
delpho/ARCO/naturepl.com; 18 Steven Kazlowski/Still Pictures;
19 Doug Allan/ naturepl.com; 21 and cover main image © 2006/
Patrick Endres/AlaskaStock.com; 22 Lynn M Stone/naturepl.com

ISBN-13: 978-0-7502-4863-1
ISBN-10: 0-7502-4863-7

Contents

Salmon live here

Salmon start and end life in a **freshwater** stream like this, but they spend most of their lives in the salty sea.

4

What is a salmon?

A salmon is a powerful fish.
There are several kinds of salmon.
Five kinds live in the Pacific Ocean
and one kind lives in the Atlantic Ocean.

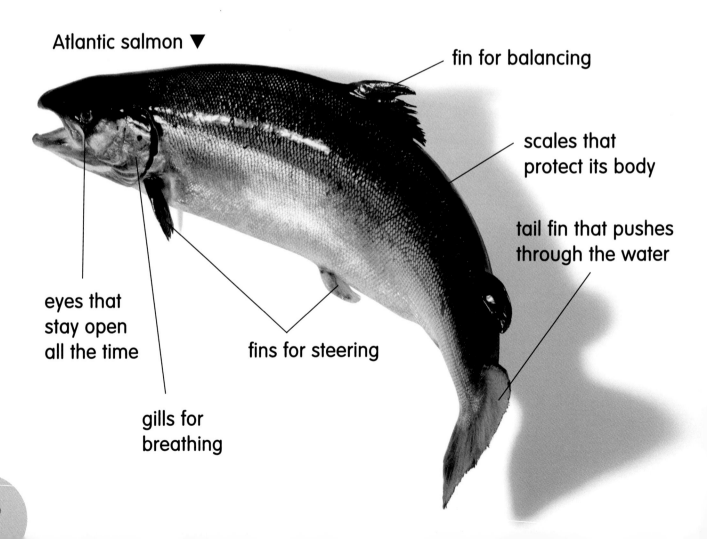

Atlantic salmon ▼

fin for balancing

scales that
protect its body

tail fin that pushes
through the water

eyes that
stay open
all the time

fins for steering

gills for
breathing

This book is about a Pacific salmon called the sockeye. The male and the female turn red on their way **upstream** to **mate**.

Making a nest

The female makes a nest on the bottom of a cold, fast-running stream. She digs a hollow with her tail in the gravel and lays hundreds of eggs.

The male covers the eggs with his **milt**
to **fertilise** them. The female hides
the eggs by flicking gravel over them.

Eggs hatch

The pea-sized eggs stay safely hidden over the winter. In early spring, they start to develop. Eyes begin to show through the eggs.

1-28
days

Tiny salmon hatch with a food sac
attached to their stomach. This is
a store of food. The salmon hide
under the gravel safe from **predators**.

Growing up

When its food sac is used up, the small **fry** pushes its way out of the gravel to find its own food. It eats tiny **plankton** in the water.

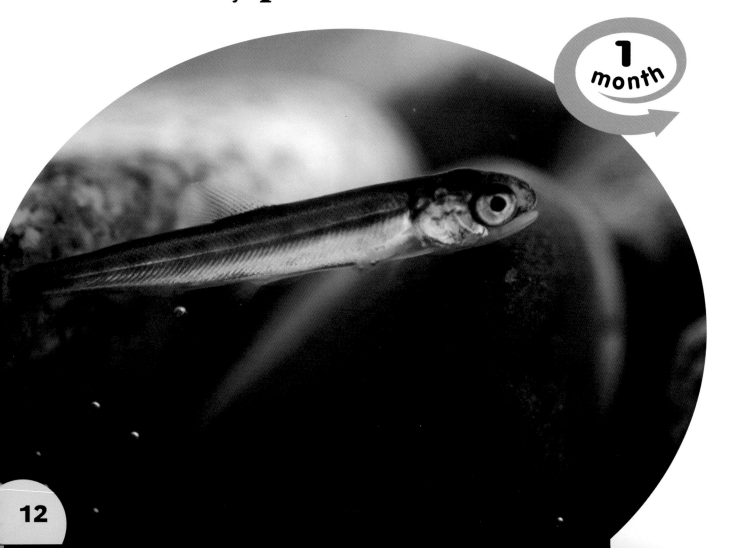

1 month

The salmon develops spots and stripes. These help it hide from hungry birds and fish. It swims downstream to a nearby lake to feed and grow.

3 months

Journey downstream

In spring, the salmon head to the sea.
There are many dangers on the way.
Some are crushed by the **turbines**
of dams that produce electricity.

Many salmon are eaten by birds and animals. Some are poisoned by polluted water from factories, farms or cities.

Reaching the estuary

The salmon reach the mouth of the river near the sea. They have grown into gleaming, silvery fish with dark blue backs.

They feed on **plankton** among the eelgrass near the shore. Here seabirds snatch many of them to eat.

Out at sea

The salmon swim out to sea. They travel hundreds of miles north to icy Arctic waters. They feed on shrimp and **plankton**. Some are caught by fishermen.

4–6 years

Hungry seals, killer whales, dolphins and sea lions also live in the Arctic seas. The salmon must try to stay clear of them.

Sea lions ▶

6 years

Journey upstream

Now the salmon are fully grown.
They swim back **upstream**
to where they were born.
They turn bright red on the way.

It is a long, tiring journey. The salmon must battle against strong currents and leap up waterfalls. Some make a tasty meal for grizzly bears.

Back home

The salmon are worn out by the time they lay their eggs. Soon after, they die. Their rotting bodies float away, filling the stream with **nutrients** for new salmon.

Salmon life cycle

Eggs
The female lays
eggs in a gravel nest.

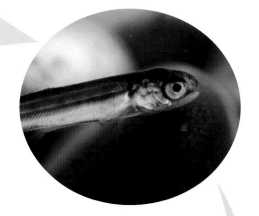

1 month
The **fry** feed
on **plankton**.

6 years
The fully-grown salmon
head **upstream** to where
they were born.

1 year
The young salmon
go out to sea.

Glossary

fertilise to make eggs ready to grow

freshwater water of rivers, streams, ponds and lakes that is not salty

fry the stage of a salmon's life after it has finished its food sac and begins to feed itself

mate when a male and female join together to produce young

milt a milky substance that male salmon spread over the eggs to **fertilise** them

nutrient a substance that helps plants and animals grow healthily

plankton tiny animals and plants that float just under water

predator an animal which feeds on other living animals

turbine an engine or machine driven by water flowing over it

upstream towards the start of a stream, in the opposite direction of the water flow

Index